33,000
EMAILS

33,000
EMAILS

33,000
EMAILS

33,000
EMAILS

33,000
EMAILS

33,000
EMAILS

33,000
EMAILS

33,000
EMAILS

33,000
EMAILS

FAKE NEWS!

FAKE NEWS!

FAKE NEWS!

FAKE NEWS!

FAKE NEWS!

FAKE NEWS!

FAKE NEWS!

FAKE NEWS!

FAKE NEWS!

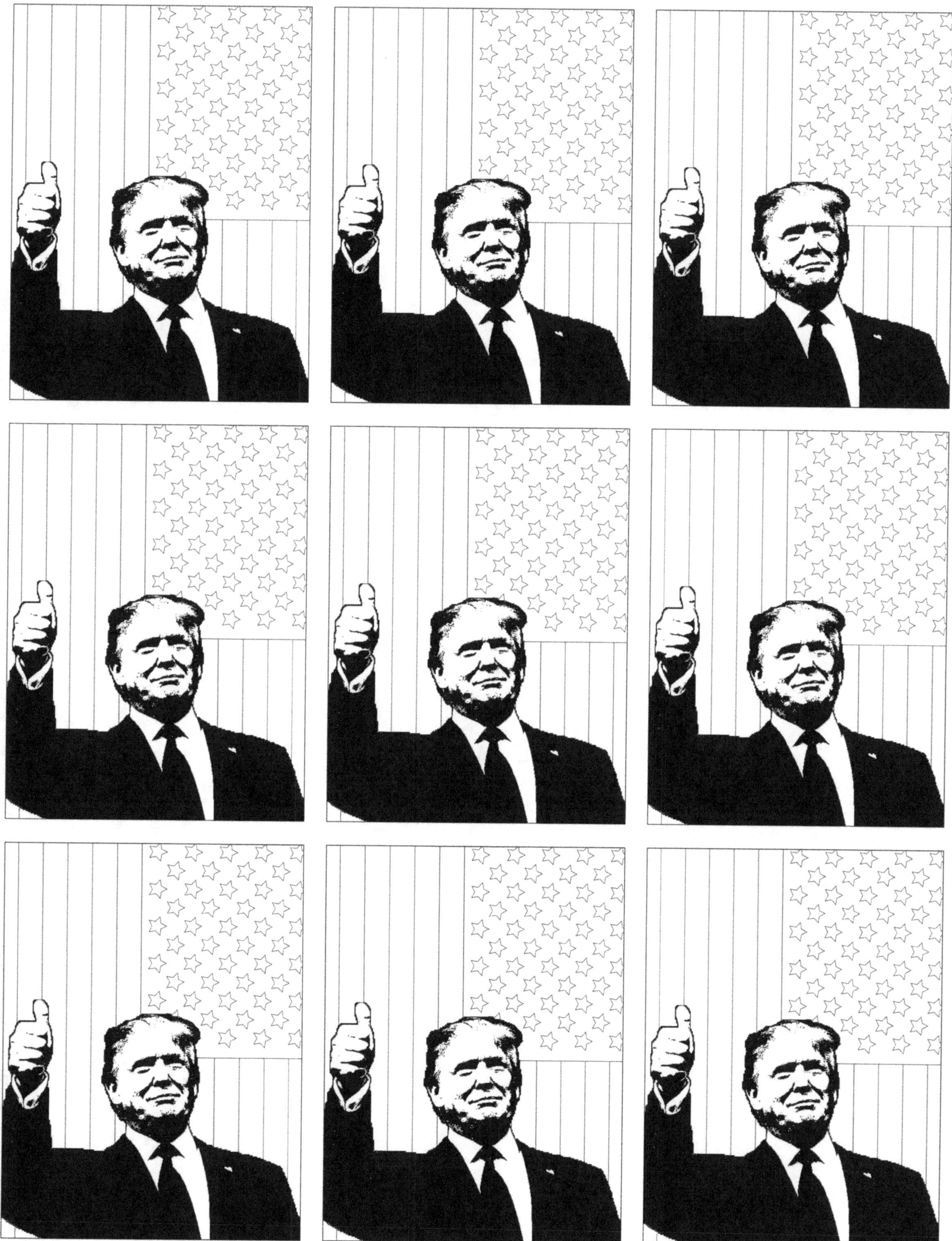

LIAR

LIAR

LIAR

LIAR

LIAR

LIAR

LIAR

LIAR

LIAR

LOCK HER UP!

LOCK HER UP!

LOCK HER UP!

LOCK HER UP!

LOCK HER UP!

LOCK HER UP!

LOCK HER UP!

LOCK HER UP!

LOCK HER UP!

#MAGA

#MAGA

#MAGA

#MAGA

#MAGA

#MAGA

#MAGA

#MAGA

#MAGA

DEEP
STATE

DEEP
STATE

DEEP
STATE

DEEP
STATE

DEEP
STATE

DEEP
STATE

DEEP
STATE

DEEP
STATE

DEEP
STATE

PSYCHOPATH

PSYCHOPATH

PSYCHOPATH

PSYCHOPATH

PSYCHOPATH

PSYCHOPATH

PSYCHOPATH

PSYCHOPATH

PSYCHOPATH

45

45

45

45

45

45

45

45

45

DRAIN
THE
SWAMP

DRAIN
THE
SWAMP

DRAIN
THE
SWAMP

DRAIN
THE
SWAMP

DRAIN
THE
SWAMP

DRAIN
THE
SWAMP

DRAIN
THE
SWAMP

DRAIN
THE
SWAMP

DRAIN
THE
SWAMP

WHY AREN'T I
50 POINTS AHEAD

WHY AREN'T I
50 POINTS AHEAD

WHY AREN'T I
50 POINTS AHEAD

WHY AREN'T I
50 POINTS AHEAD

WHY AREN'T I
50 POINTS AHEAD

WHY AREN'T I
50 POINTS AHEAD

WHY AREN'T I
50 POINTS AHEAD

WHY AREN'T I
50 POINTS AHEAD

WHY AREN'T I
50 POINTS AHEAD

DON'T WORRY, WE'LL BUILD THE WALL
MAKE AMERICA GREAT AGAIN

DON'T WORRY, WE'LL BUILD THE WALL
MAKE AMERICA GREAT AGAIN

DON'T WORRY, WE'LL BUILD THE WALL
MAKE AMERICA GREAT AGAIN

DON'T WORRY, WE'LL BUILD THE WALL
MAKE AMERICA GREAT AGAIN

DON'T WORRY, WE'LL BUILD THE WALL
MAKE AMERICA GREAT AGAIN

DON'T WORRY, WE'LL BUILD THE WALL
MAKE AMERICA GREAT AGAIN

DON'T WORRY, WE'LL BUILD THE WALL
MAKE AMERICA GREAT AGAIN

DON'T WORRY, WE'LL BUILD THE WALL
MAKE AMERICA GREAT AGAIN

DON'T WORRY, WE'LL BUILD THE WALL
MAKE AMERICA GREAT AGAIN

HANNITY

HANNITY

HANNITY

HANNITY

HANNITY

HANNITY

HANNITY

HANNITY

EVIL

EVIL

EVIL

EVIL

EVIL

EVIL

EVIL

EVIL

EVIL

RACIST
HOMOPHOBIC
XENOPHOBIC
ISLAMAPHOBIC

RACIST
HOMOPHOBIC
XENOPHOBIC
ISLAMAPHOBIC

RACIST
HOMOPHOBIC
XENOPHOBIC
ISLAMAPHOBIC

RACIST
HOMOPHOBIC
XENOPHOBIC
ISLAMAPHOBIC

RACIST
HOMOPHOBIC
XENOPHOBIC
ISLAMAPHOBIC

RACIST
HOMOPHOBIC
XENOPHOBIC
ISLAMAPHOBIC

RACIST
HOMOPHOBIC
XENOPHOBIC
ISLAMAPHOBIC

RACIST
HOMOPHOBIC
XENOPHOBIC
ISLAMAPHOBIC

RACIST
HOMOPHOBIC
XENOPHOBIC
ISLAMAPHOBIC

THE GREAT ONE
THE GREAT ONE
THE GREAT ONE
THE GREAT ONE
THE GREAT ONE
THE GREAT ONE
THE GREAT ONE
THE GREAT ONE
THE GREAT ONE

MERRY CHRISTMAS
Merry Christmas
TRUMP
Grand Rapids, Michigan
MAKE AMERICA GREAT AGAIN!

MERRY CHRISTMAS
Merry Christmas
TRUMP
Grand Rapids, Michigan
MAKE AMERICA GREAT AGAIN!

MERRY CHRISTMAS
Merry Christmas
TRUMP
Grand Rapids, Michigan
MAKE AMERICA GREAT AGAIN!

MERRY CHRISTMAS
Merry Christmas
TRUMP
Grand Rapids, Michigan
MAKE AMERICA GREAT AGAIN!

MERRY CHRISTMAS
Merry Christmas
TRUMP
Grand Rapids, Michigan
MAKE AMERICA GREAT AGAIN!

MERRY CHRISTMAS
Merry Christmas
TRUMP
Grand Rapids, Michigan
MAKE AMERICA GREAT AGAIN!

MERRY CHRISTMAS
Merry Christmas
TRUMP
Grand Rapids, Michigan
MAKE AMERICA GREAT AGAIN!

MERRY CHRISTMAS
Merry Christmas
TRUMP
Grand Rapids, Michigan
MAKE AMERICA GREAT AGAIN!

MERRY CHRISTMAS
Merry Christmas
TRUMP
Grand Rapids, Michigan
MAKE AMERICA GREAT AGAIN!

MAKE
AMERICA
GREAT
AGAIN

MAKE
AMERICA
GREAT
AGAIN

MAKE
AMERICA
GREAT
AGAIN

MAKE
AMERICA
GREAT
AGAIN

MAKE
AMERICA
GREAT
AGAIN

MAKE
AMERICA
GREAT
AGAIN

MAKE
AMERICA
GREAT
AGAIN

MAKE
AMERICA
GREAT
AGAIN

MAKE
AMERICA
GREAT
AGAIN

WHAT DIFFERENCE AT THIS POINT DOES IT MAKE

WHAT DIFFERENCE AT THIS POINT DOES IT MAKE

WHAT DIFFERENCE AT THIS POINT DOES IT MAKE

WHAT DIFFERENCE AT THIS POINT DOES IT MAKE

WHAT DIFFERENCE AT THIS POINT DOES IT MAKE

WHAT DIFFERENCE AT THIS POINT DOES IT MAKE

WHAT DIFFERENCE AT THIS POINT DOES IT MAKE

WHAT DIFFERENCE AT THIS POINT DOES IT MAKE

WHAT DIFFERENCE AT THIS POINT DOES IT MAKE

BOMB THE HELL OUT OF THEM

BOMB THE HELL OUT OF THEM

BOMB THE HELL OUT OF THEM

BOMB THE HELL OUT OF THEM

BOMB THE HELL OUT OF THEM

BOMB THE HELL OUT OF THEM

BOMB THE HELL OUT OF THEM

BOMB THE HELL OUT OF THEM

BOMB THE HELL OUT OF THEM

FLOTUS
FLOTUS
FLOTUS
FLOTUS
FLOTUS
FLOTUS
FLOTUS
FLOTUS
FLOTUS

#JOBS

#JOBS

#JOBS

#JOBS

#JOBS

#JOBS

#JOBS

#JOBS

#JOBS

CRIMINAL

CRIMINAL

CRIMINAL

CRIMINAL

CRIMINAL

CRIMINAL

CRIMINAL

CRIMINAL

CRIMINAL

YOU'RE FIRED
YOU'RE FIRED
YOU'RE FIRED
YOU'RE FIRED
YOU'RE FIRED
YOU'RE FIRED
YOU'RE FIRED
YOU'RE FIRED
YOU'RE FIRED

www.ingramcontent.com/pod-product-compliance
Lightning Source LLC
Chambersburg PA
CBHW082332270726
48658CB00018B/3248